Date Due

Fundamental

Gymnastics coaches Linda
Wallenberg Bragg and
Scott Gay and the following
athletes were photographed
for this book:
  Jill Ames,
  Tony Aretz,
  Nikki Benedict,
  Kristy Bowman,
  Matt Bulger,
  Heidi Cady,
  Sara Dunphy,
  R.J. Emery,
  Beth Flaherty,
  Andrew Gagner,
  Andrew Hackman,
  Christian Hyun,
  Nicholas Johnson,
  Lori Lehman,
  Pat Nelson,
  Adam Reichow,
  Cathy Sohn,
  Stacy Swigart,
  Mark Tundel,
  Kelli Ueland.

AAI
AMERICAN

Fundamental
GYMNASTICS

Linda
Wallenberg
Bragg

Photographs by
Andy King

Lerner Publications Company ● Minneapolis

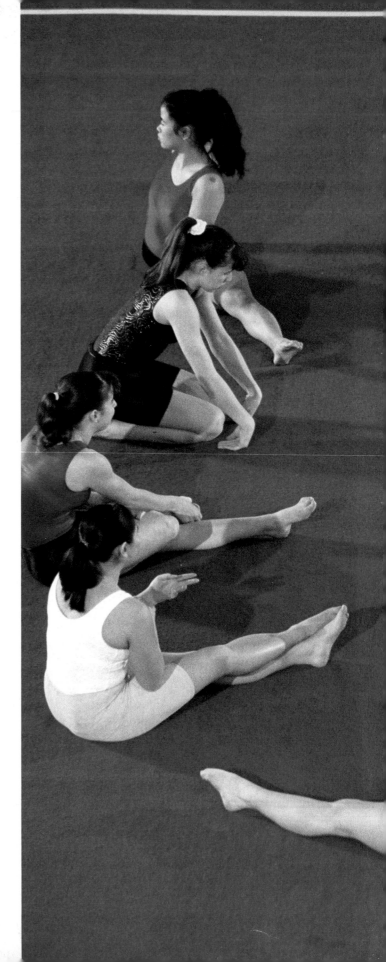

For my mom and dad who've always been there behind me, for Glenn who is always there beside me, and for Carina and Robby who show the way in front of me.

The Fundamental Sports series was conceptualized by editor Julie Jensen, designed by graphic artist Michael Tacheny, and composed on a Macintosh computer by Robert Mauzy. The Fundamental Sports series was designed in conjunction with the Beginning Sports series to offer young athletes a basic understanding of various sports at two reading levels.

Photo Acknowledgments
Photographs are reproduced with the permission of: p. 7, Scala/Art Resource, N.Y.; p. 8, The Bettmann Archive; p. 9 (top), UPI/Bettmann; p. 9 (bottom), ALLSPORT/Steve Powell; p. 10, ALLSPORT; p. 11, ALLSPORT/Doug Pensinger; p. 14, ALLSPORT/ Tony Duffy; p. 63, ALLSPORT/Chris Cole; p. 74 (top), ALLSPORT/Gary M. Prior.
Copyright © 1995 by Lerner Publications Company

Lerner Publications Company
A Division of Lerner Publishing Group
241 First Avenue North
Minneapolis, MN 55401 U.S.A.

Website address: www.lernerbooks.com

Library of Congress Cataloging-in-Publication Data

Bragg, Linda Wallenberg.
    Fundamental gymnastics / Linda Wallenberg Bragg ;
  photographs by Andy King.
      p.   cm.
    Includes bibliographical references (p.) and index.
    ISBN 0–8225–3453–3 :
    1. Gymnastics—Juvenile literature. [1. Gymnastics.]
I. King, Andy, ill. II. Title.
GV461.B716 1995
796.44—dc20   94–40770

Manufactured in the United States of America
3 4 5 6 7 8 - CPG - 05 04 03 02 01 00

Contents

Chapter 1.0

HOW THIS SPORT GOT STARTED

Imagine tiptoeing on a 4-inch wide piece of wood. In less than one second, you lift your arms and propel your body upward into a tight little tucked ball. For a split second you see the ceiling. Now—quick!—you squeeze your ankles tight. In a flash, that skinny piece of wood is under your feet again. You did it! You landed safely—on the **balance beam**.

Such is the life of a gymnast. Gymnasts perform physical activities that require strength, balance, and body control. If this excitement appeals to you, you're probably one of thousands of young people, girls and boys, all over the world, who have fallen in love with this dynamic and challenging sport.

Gymnasts were featured in some ancient Greek artworks, such as this vase.

7

Gymnastics combines the thrill of turning your body upside down with the artistry of dancing. A gymnast tries to perform every move to absolute perfection. In fact, because of its beauty, some people think gymnastics is more of a performing art than a sport.

Plato, a Greek philosopher, said:

*God, I should say,
has given men two arts,
music and gymnastics.*

Plato believed that music educated the mind and gymnastics trained the body.

The History of Gymnastics

Gymnastics has been around for thousands of years. Most people believe it was started by the Greeks, who loved physical activity. The Greeks, in fact, held the first Olympic Games more than 2,000 years ago. We don't know exactly how the Greeks started doing gymnastics, but on ancient Greek paintings and vases there are pictures of athletes jumping, running, lifting and throwing weights, climbing ropes, wrestling, and tumbling. The word "gymnastics" was used for any physical activity that was performed in a training center called a gymnasium.

Friedrich Jahn from Germany is known as the father of gymnastics. In 1811 he built an outdoor gymnastics center. He made crude pieces of equipment and used them to teach students gymnastics moves and to develop their strength. His was the first gymnastics club, and clubs are still very important in training young gymnasts. Groups of gymnasts train together in clubs.

Friedrich Jahn formed the first club for gymnastics in 1811 in Germany.

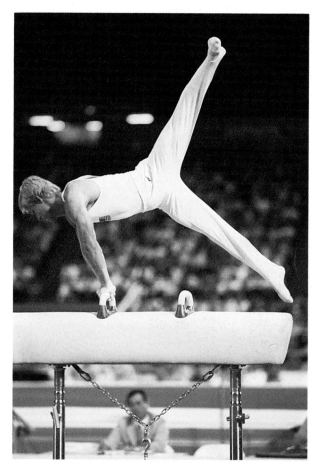

Left, Mitsuo Tsukahara of Japan was famous throughout the world when he competed during the 1970s. Below, Bart Conner's clean technique helped the United States team win the gold medal at the 1984 Olympic Games.

Between 1850 and 1900, gymnastics became popular throughout the entire world. In fact, gymnastics was one of nine original sports in the first modern Olympics, held in Athens, Greece, in 1896. Only men competed in the first modern Olympics. They performed on six pieces of equipment, called **apparatus:** the **parallel bars, horizontal bar, rings, pommel horse, vault,** and ropes. (They competed in rope climbing instead of the **floor exercise,** as gymnasts do now.) The Olympic Games encouraged people who were interested in gymnastics competition to develop equipment standards, rules, and regulations. The World Gymnastics Championships began in 1901 and still take place.

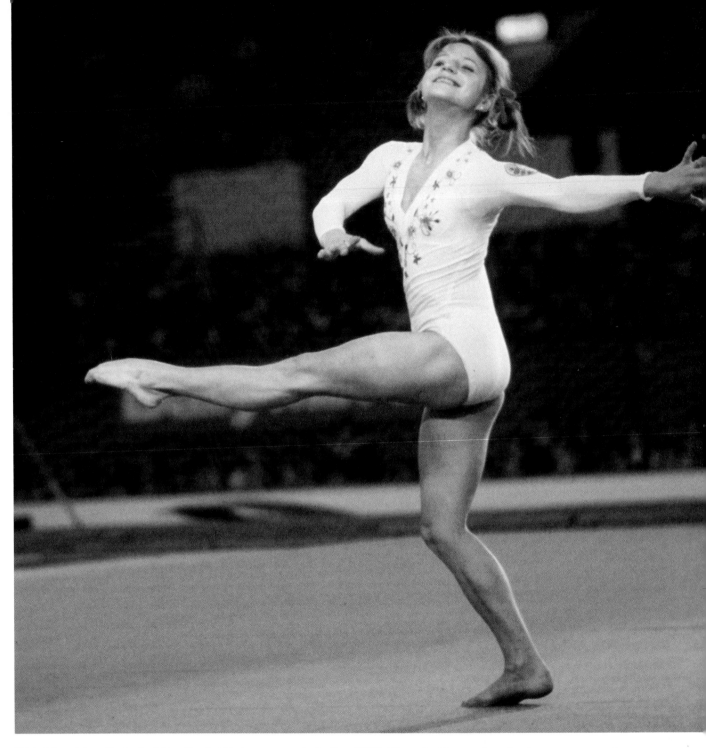

Watching Olga Korbut of the Soviet Union compete in the 1972 Olympic Games inspired many youngsters to learn gymnastics.

At first, girls weren't encouraged to take part in gymnastics. Some people didn't think women had the physical strength and power for such a sport. However, women's gymnastics team competition was introduced in the 1928 Olympics. At the Olympic Games in 1952, the female gymnasts from the Soviet Union dazzled the crowd. Soon, special equipment was developed for women's events, and individual competition in women's gymnastics began.

For the next 20 years, women and girls made their mark in the gymnastics world. When the 1960 Olympics were broadcast on television, many people were amazed by the beauty of women's gymnastics. By the 1970s, there were more famous female gymnasts than male. Even people who had never watched a gymnastics meet had heard of Olga Korbut from the Soviet Union, Nadia Comaneci from Romania, and Cathy Rigby from the United States.

Gymnastics became very popular in the 1960s and 1970s. The Japanese men and the Soviet Union women won most of the major competitions. But soon, world-class gymnasts were German, Hungarian, Romanian, and—by the 1980s and 1990s—American.

This book will introduce you to the basics of the sport of gymnastics. Just like any other sport, gymnastics requires you to train your body. But it also requires you to train your mind and your emotions.

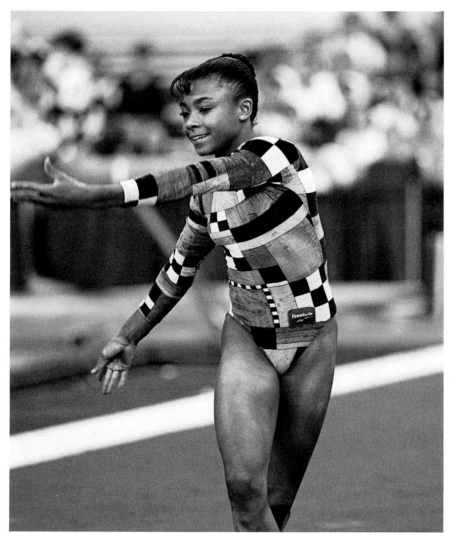

Dominique Dawes burst onto the American gymnastics scene in the 1990s. She was a member of the U.S. Olympic team that won a gold medal in the 1996 Olympics.

BASICS

Anyone can learn to do gymnastics. It takes many years, however, for someone to develop into a competitive gymnast. The best gymnasts usually started taking gymnastics lessons when they were three to five years old.

In the beginning lessons, the coach mainly works on developing a gymnast's coordination, balance, and flexibility. Many young children are either naturally strong or naturally flexible. The best gymnasts are both.

Toddlers work on pointing their toes and stretching their muscles. They will even start tumbling. By the time beginning gymnasts start school, they are usually working on gymnastics apparatus and developing strength in specific muscles. A lot of the time is spent learning tumbling skills. But the apparatus are becoming the big challenge.

What Does a Gymnast Wear?

Specific rules tell gymnasts, both male and female, what they can wear when competing. If a gymnast doesn't follow the rules of proper dress in competition, he or she will lose some points (called a deduction). Team members often wear the same type and color of uniform to display their unity.

Traditions are a big part of gymnastics dress. Although it is no longer required, boys have traditionally worn white pants when performing on pommel horse, parallel bars, horizontal bar, and rings. For vault and floor exercise, they wear shorts.

Most coaches have rules about what gymnasts should wear when practicing. Above all, the gymnast's clothing can't restrict movement. Most gymnasts wear one-piece leotards. When a coach is physically assisting (spotting) a gymnast, the clothing must not hinder the coach. That's why most coaches don't allow T-shirts and do require that long hair be tied back. Some gymnasts wear gymnastic slippers, and others prefer to perform in their bare feet.

13

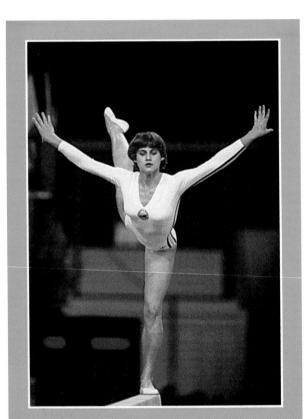

Nadia Comaneci competed for Romania during the 1970s.

A Sport of Constant Change

Gymnasts are constantly looking for new ways to perform old skills, or they're thinking up completely new skills! Part of a gymnast's score is for originality, and the more original a routine is, the more interested the judges and spectators are. Skills are usually named after the gymnasts who first perform them.

*For example, the **tsukahara** vault is named after a Japanese gymnast, Mitsuo Tsukahara, who competed in the 1970s. The **comaneci** dismount on the uneven parallel bars is named after legendary Romanian gymnast Nadia Comaneci, who stunned the world in the 1970s with her amazing string of perfect routines.*

Parallel Bars (boys)

Rings (boys)

Pommel Horse (boys)

Gymnastics Events

There are six events in boys' gymnastics: floor exercise, vault, pommel horse, rings, parallel bars, and horizontal bar. Girls compete in four events: floor exercise, vault, **uneven parallel bars,** and balance beam.

Boys' and girls' events have many similarities. That's why, in a lot of classes, boys and girls can learn some of the same skills together. Boys and girls both compete on the floor exercise

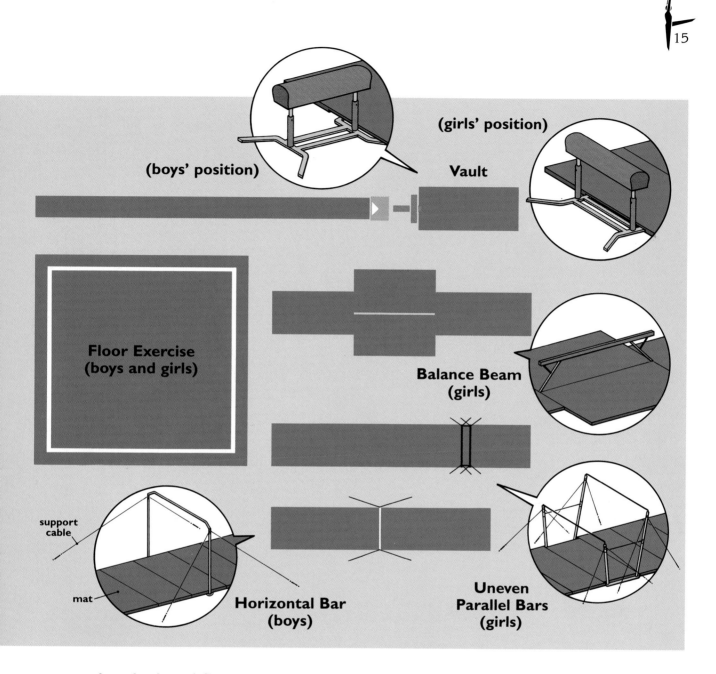

(boys' position)

(girls' position)

Vault

Floor Exercise
(boys and girls)

Balance Beam
(girls)

support
cable

mat

Horizontal Bar
(boys)

Uneven
Parallel Bars
(girls)

mat, but the boys' floor routine emphasizes tumbling and isn't performed to music. Girls' floor routines are performed to music and include tumbling and dance moves.

Boys and girls both compete on the vault. However, the girls vault over the horse with it *sideways* while the boys vault over the horse *lengthwise*.

For boys, the bars are side by side, or parallel. Girls compete on the un-

even parallel bars—one bar is higher than the other.

Although the boys' events have no direct counterpart to the girls' balance beam, many people believe the beam is similar to the pommel horse. Both events present a great challenge to the gymnast just to stay on the apparatus. For many gymnasts, these events require much longer practice periods than do the others.

Boys' Events

● *Floor Exercise*

The gymnast has a standard number of seconds in which to perform sequences of tumbling skills, called a routine. The routine must show the gymnast's strength, timing, control, dynamic power, and precision.

Mark is doing a basic floor exercise skill called a **front handspring**. This skill requires him to spring forward and upward into the air with his body slightly arched and leaning forward.

Mark starts from a stretched stand. He takes a quick run and then places his hands shoulder-width apart on the floor. He kicks his rear leg into the air and then extends his front leg. His shoulders **block** as his hips pass

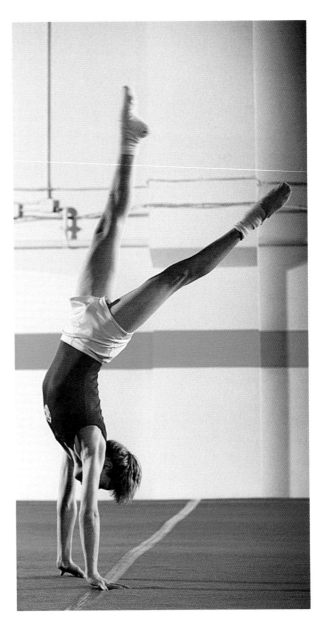

through the upside-down position. This causes his body to rise. The landing can be on one foot and then the other foot, or on both feet together.

Men used to perform their floor exercise routines on bare floors or on strips of mats with very little padding. Now, floor exercise equipment is more so-

phisticated. For most competition and advanced training, the floor consists of either foam blocks or springs mounted under at least one layer of wood. Another layer of thick foam is placed on top of the wood, with a piece of carpet measuring 40 feet by 40 feet on top of the foam. This type of floor, called a rebound or **spring floor**, helps protect the gymnast from injury.

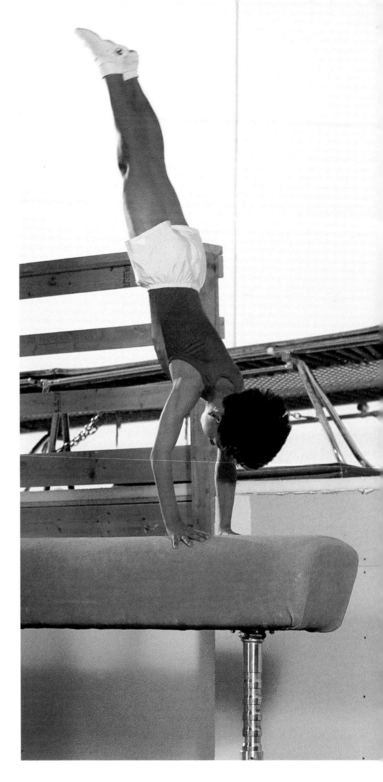

● *Vault*

The vault is also called the horse. Boys use it positioned lengthwise. The vault is a padded wooden structure 3 feet, 7 inches high. The routine the gymnast performs over a vault is also called a vault, and it takes just four or five seconds to complete.

A springboard is placed in front of the vault. When training, gymnasts often use a mini-trampoline instead of a springboard. Christian is using a mini-tramp. A long, cushioned runway leads to the springboard.

Christian begins somewhere near the end of the runway. First, he takes an explosive run and pushes off the mini-trampoline. **Preflight** is the term for the entry onto the vault itself. The gymnast should only touch the horse for a fraction of a second before thrusting off it.

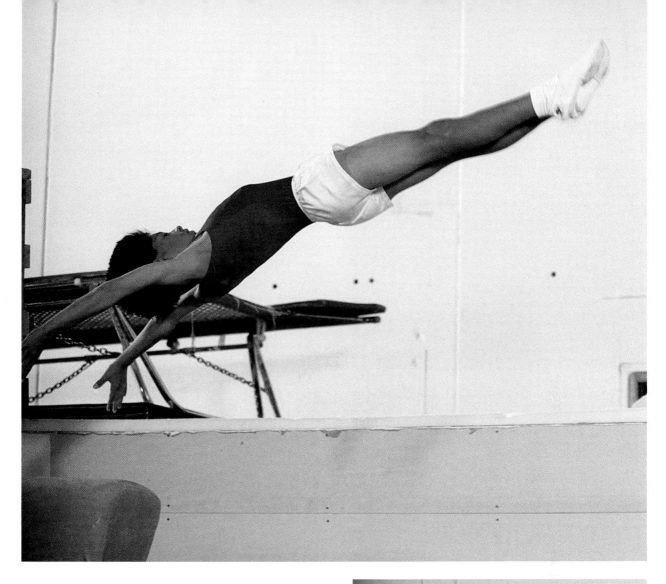

Next comes the **postflight,** which usually includes a flip or a **twist** or both.
Then Christian does a controlled landing onto protective landing mats on the
other side of the vault.

● Pommel Horse

The pommel horse, or side horse, is a padded structure that has two handles on it called pommels. The pommel horse is 3 feet, 7 inches high. The pommels are used to support the gymnast's weight while he swings from side to side and forward and back. The gymnast's hands have to grasp and re-grasp the pommels to allow his legs to pass beneath his hands.

Christian, at left, is beginning to learn how to travel on the pommel horse. This event is especially difficult, as you can imagine. In fact, young gymnasts such as Andrew, below, often begin to learn pommel horse moves on a piece of training equipment called a mushroom. Andrew is practicing his **circles** on the mushroom. Eventually he will use this skill on the pommel horse.

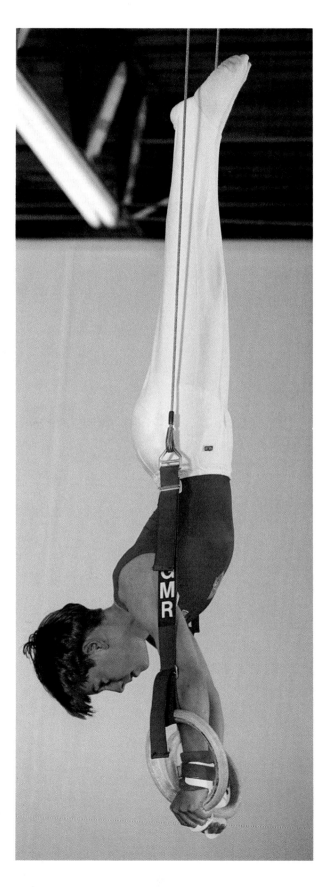

● *Still Rings*

The still rings (rings for short) are completely circular, made of wood or fiberglass, and are suspended by straps from a steel frame. The rings are about 1 foot, 7½ inches apart and hang about 8 feet, 3 inches above the ground. The gymnast does circle and swinging movements. He also stops occasionally to show control, as Pat is doing in his handstand at left. The gymnast is also expected to show strength, as Nick is demonstrating below with a back lever.

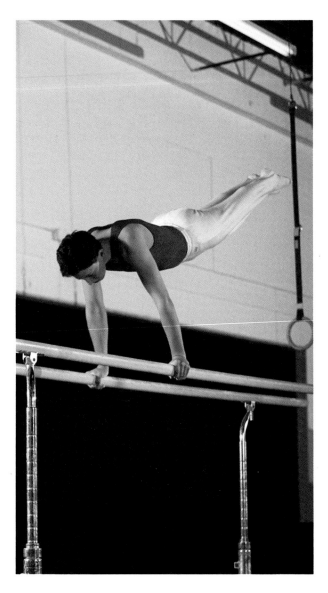

● *Parallel Bars*

The parallel bars are two wood or fiber-glass bars, 11 feet, 6 inches long and about 1½ feet apart. They are supported on **uprights** mounted on a single steel base. The bars are 5 feet, 6 inches above the ground. Most of the gymnast's movements are done above the bars. The gymnast must swing and keep his routine flowing. Tony is demonstrating good swing technique.

● *Horizontal Bar*

Perhaps the most thrilling of the boys' events is the horizontal bar, or high bar. This is an 8-foot long steel bar placed about 8 feet above the floor. The bar must be high enough to allow the gymnast to swing all the way around it with circling movements. The high bar is often lowered for beginning gymnasts who are just learning and getting used to its height.

Christian is demonstrating the basic swing used in high bar work, called a **giant swing**. When doing a giant, the gymnast holds onto the bar with both hands circling around the bar. Christian extends and then tightens his body during this maneuver.

Girls' Events

● *Floor Exercise*

In the floor exercise routine, a female gymnast must show good technique with pointed toes and near perfect body line. Sara illustrates this attention to detail in her **front walkover**.

The floor exercise routine must have a balance of tumbling and dance, and it must be choreographed perfectly to music. The entire routine must be completed within a 1½-minute time limit.

A floor exercise routine requires a great deal of endurance. The last **tumbling pass** should be as difficult and exciting as the first.

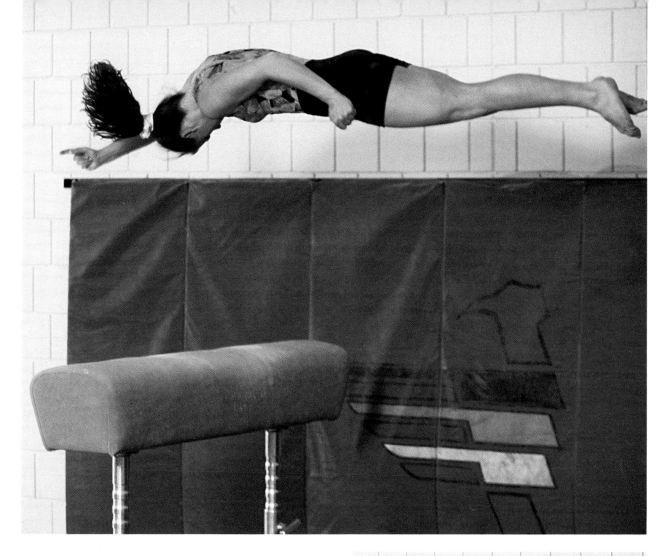

● *Vault*

The girls' vault event is similar to the boys' except that the vault is turned sideways rather than lengthwise. The vaulting apparatus, or horse, is 3 feet, 7 inches high. Girls and boys do basically the same vaults. Stacy is demonstrating a vault.

After she sprints down the runway, she hits the board, enters the preflight phase, and pushes off the horse. Stacy twists on the postflight. She tries to **stick** the landing, which means landing without taking any steps to regain her balance.

28

Heidi injured her knee. After it healed, she began doing gymnastics again. She wears a brace to protect her knee from injury.

● *Uneven Parallel Bars*

The uneven parallel bars (or asymmetric bars) are two bars slotted into two sets of steel uprights. Each bar is the same length as the boys' horizontal bar, and one bar is higher than the other. One bar is 7 feet, 6 inches above the floor and the other is 4 feet, 11 inches. Some people think that the uneven parallel bars are the most dynamic of all the girls' events, combining the skill of the parallel bars with the thrill of the horizontal bar. In recent years, many of

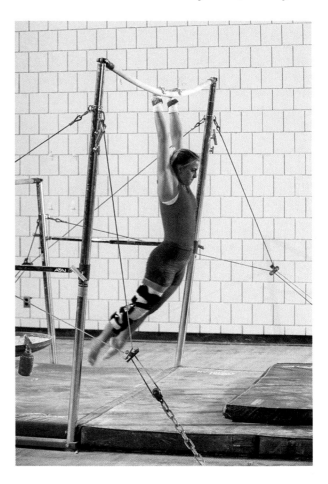

the skills that were once thought only possible on the high bar are being performed on the uneven parallel bars.

A gymnast on the uneven parallel bars moves in a continuous flow of swinging and circling. Heidi demonstrates this with her giant swing.

● *Balance Beam*

Originally, and until just recently, the balance beam was always made of wood. Now some are made of aluminum. The beam is usually padded, with a suede covering. It is 4 inches wide and 16 feet, 5 inches long. The beam is 3 feet, 11 inches above the floor for competition. It may be set lower for practice. The gymnast's routine on the balance beam can't be longer than 1 minute and 30 seconds. Timing begins at the moment the gymnast's feet leave the floor in a **mount**. A **dismount** completes her routine.

The balance beam was first used only for balancing and posing. Sara, at left, is showing precision and balance in this **handstand**. Now, the gymnast must also dance on the beam. And that's not all! The gymnast must also do a series of tumbling skills such as the back walkover Jill is doing, below.

Building Blocks

Learning to do gymnastics is like climbing up a ladder. The most successful and safest way to learn skills is slowly and with progression. This means that each skill should build on the last—just like climbing up a ladder one rung at a time.

Of course, some gymnasts progress faster than others. There are people who seem to be naturally gifted in gymnastics. Just as some people can reach the top of a ladder by skipping rungs, some gymnasts can also skip a few steps in the learning process. However, every gymnast must understand and use several key ideas.

First, gymnasts must learn proper body awareness. A gymnast must know exactly where she is in the air while flying off a 4-inch beam. A gymnast also must understand proper body alignment. A gymnast's body flips and twists more cleanly and safely if every part of the body is in line. Knowing the correct alignment for each skill helps keep a gymnast safe.

Also, gymnasts must be prepared for falls. Falling is inevitable while learning and performing skills. Sometimes, what looks like a fall at the end of a routine may just be the dismount. In any case, knowing how to recover from a fall and how to perform a proper dismount landing is an essential part of doing gymnastics. Gymnasts practice skills that help them land safely.

Other Equipment

In addition to the apparatus, gymnasts need equipment to make their workout and competitive routines comfortable and safe.

Most gymnasts use chalk (actually magnesium carbonate) on their hands and sometimes their feet to ensure a good grip on the apparatus. The chalk helps keep hands and feet from getting sweaty. Sometimes coaches and gymnasts put the chalk directly on the apparatus to guard against slipping.

*Many gymnasts also use **grips**, or handguards, when working on the rings or the various types of bars. There is a lot of friction between the palms of the gymnast's hands and the apparatus. Without grips, the gymnast's hands might blister or tear, making it very painful for him or her to work the bars.*

Landing mats are absolutely necessary. These mats are 4 to 10 inches high and often have a 1-inch base mat underneath for further protection. Landing mats are used to cushion and protect the gymnast when he or she is doing a dismount.

National and international gymnastics organizations set safety standards for the apparatus and mats, and even suggest distances the apparatus should be placed from each other. Some equipment may be adjusted by gymnasts to conform better to their body sizes for maximum safety. Coaches and gymnasts must be committed to safety. They should check the apparatus often to be sure they are stable and correctly set up.

One basic concept of gymnastics is that a gymnast's body moves most effectively in the air when it's in one of three positions: **tuck, pike,** and **layout**.

When Stacy's knees are tucked in close so that her body resembles a ball, she will rotate faster than if her body is stretched out. When gymnasts are first learning to flip in the air, the coach usually teaches this tuck position.

As gymnasts advance, they learn to straighten out their legs and perform in a pike or layout position. In a pike position, the gymnast bends at the hips but keeps his or her legs straight. In a layout position, the gymnast's entire body is in a straight line. In these positions, the body moves more slowly through the air. Many people feel these positions are much more pleasing to watch than the tucked position.

Once you have learned the layout position, your coach may teach you to twist your body either half or all the way around as you do a maneuver. When that happens, you're on your way to being an advanced gymnast!

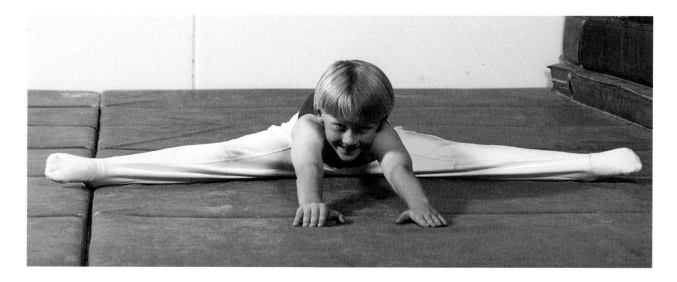

A gymnast needs to bend well—like a Gumby® doll. Gymnasts especially need flexible legs, backs, and shoulders. The **pancake** Adam is doing shows his leg and back flexibility. Although some gymnasts are born more flexible than others, all gymnasts must constantly work on maintaining or increasing their flexibility. Even ankle flexibility is important. In gymnastics, stretched ankles and pointed toes look better than flexed ankles.

Stretched ankles and pointed toes result in a clean line.

Flexing your ankles breaks the pleasing body line and isn't good technique.

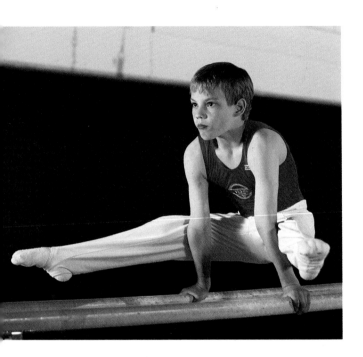

Not only should gymnasts be flexible, they must also be very strong. Events such as the uneven parallel bars for girls and the still rings for boys show the key role strength plays in gymnastics.

Most coaches have gymnasts spend time building their strength during practice sessions. This strength building is called conditioning. Sometimes practicing the basic skills of gymnastics is part of the conditioning sessions, but gymnasts also do specific exercises that help them develop strength in different parts of their bodies.

For example, Matt's **straddle** hold, left, shows strength in his arms, legs, and abdomen. Gymnasts often do **V-ups** instead of regular sit-ups to develop strength in their stomachs. Parallel bar **dips** and the push-ups Lori is doing, below, develop arm strength.

Tumbling Basics

When girls and boys first start gymnastics lessons, they learn the basic skills of tumbling.

● *Handstand*

The handstand is, perhaps, the most important skill in gymnastics. Mark, at left, is doing a handstand in his parallel bars routine. In a handstand, the hands, not the feet, are the sole support of the gymnast's body. The handstand position is a part of every boys' and girls' event. As Lori's handstand shows, the gymnast's body must be held in an absolutely straight line. In the past, gymnasts didn't pay much attention to proper body line and did handstands with an arched, or banana, back. Allowing the back to curve, however, is now considered poor and inefficient technique.

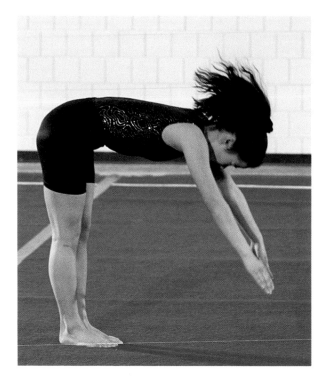

● *Roll*

The first gymnastics move many children learn—often in their own back-yards—is called a **roll**. Rolls can be performed both forward and backward. Once the basic rolls are mastered, variations can be added.

Notice how Cathy is changing her body from a stretched position to a small ball-like position—in other words, a tuck. She rolls on her rounded back as her legs lift up and over her head. Once the roll is completed, Cathy stands up into the stretched or finished position with her arms extended. Rolls can also be performed on the balance beam.

● *Cartwheel*

Not only can gymnasts tumble forward and backward, they can also tumble sideways. Many people have experienced the joy of doing a **cartwheel,** even without lessons.

Sara starts from a stand, kicks her lead leg, and then lunges forward and rotates sideways from her hip joint until her lead hand contacts the mat. Then she kicks her legs into the air, her straight one first, into a straddle position. Her legs remain straight throughout the move.

When she's upside down, Sara's body looks like the spokes of a wheel. Her finishing stand looks just like the beginning. A cartwheel can be performed on one arm or even without touching the floor. A cartwheel without using the hands is called an aerial cartwheel.

Left or Right?

If you're learning to do a cartwheel for the first time, how do you know which hand to put down first—your right or your left? Do you put down your right because you're right-handed? Not necessarily!

When people write, they are naturally either right- or left-handed. In the same way, people usually are right- or left-side tumblers. However, you may write with your right hand but find you prefer to do cartwheels with your left hand first!

In advanced competitive gymnastics, it really doesn't matter which side you prefer. But in the early training, coaches will often encourage gymnasts to learn the basic skills on both sides. When skills are done in combination, it might be easier for the gymnast to have the option of tumbling left or right. Once a gymnast has a preferred side, it's often hard for that person to change.

● *Roundoff*

The **roundoff** is the main skill that leads to most backward tumbling combinations. Doing the roundoff correctly is the key to becoming a strong, dynamic backward tumbler. The roundoff transfers forward power into backward power. You might call it a change-of-direction skill.

Lori begins her roundoff with a quick run into a **hurdle** or hop step. Then, as if for a cartwheel, she reaches through the **lunge** position and puts down both hands simultaneously. As she pushes through her arms and chest, she brings her feet together. When she is upside down, her body rotates over the top so that she snaps down facing the opposite direction from where she began.

● Handspring

Handsprings can be performed both backward and forward. The **back handspring** is sometimes called a flip-flop or a flick-flack.

Beth starts in a stretched, standing position. She pushes off from her feet and leans backward. She lands on her hands, flips her feet over her head, and then lands on her feet again. She must use explosive power to boost her body high into the air.

Forward or Backward?

Many coaches teach a back handspring and a back somersault before the front versions. Very young gymnasts may be less fearful of tumbling forward rather than of tumbling backward because they can see where they're headed. But it's easier to land a backward skill than it is a forward skill because you can see your hands or your feet land. Think about landing on a 4-inch-wide balance beam! In a forward move, the landing is called a blind landing because you cannot see your feet land before you are there!

● *Somersault*

People often call a **somersault** a "flip." Somersaults are particularly fun to do because as you rotate in the air, for a moment, you feel like you're flying. A somersault requires good spatial awareness—knowing where you are in the air at all times. Somersaults aren't just used in floor exercise routines. A somersault is often used during a dismount, which is the skill done to leave an apparatus.

A somersault can be done backward, forward, or sideward. A roundoff or a back handspring on the floor is often done just before a somersault.

Pat demonstrates a front somersault.

He starts in a stretched position for the takeoff, lifts his arms, and reaches with an explosive thrust. As his arms rise, he pushes off with both feet up into the air. At the top of the lift, you can see that Pat is in a tuck, similar to that for a forward roll. His body will then rotate all the way around and he lands on his feet. His hands never touch the floor.

Whether you do a front or back somersault, you can add many variations. Your body can be tucked, piked, or in the layout position. If you are in the layout position, you can add a half, full, double-full, or even a triple-full twist. The somersault is truly an exciting move!

The Dance Component

As mentioned earlier, music and dance are a big part of girls' floor exercise routines. Dance is also a large part of the balance beam event. For both events, the gymnast must perform turns, jumps, and leaps. She should also include runs, walks, and skips, which connect the tumbling and the dance. Fluid use of the arms and body, including **body waves,** enhances a floor exercise performance. Gymnasts spend almost as much time and effort learning dance skills as they do learning tumbling skills.

Dance movements in the floor exercise event must be done in harmony with the music and should fit the style of the gymnast. The movements may come from ballet, modern, ethnic, folk, or jazz dance. No matter what the style, the dance used in gymnastics routines must show good form.

● *Turns*

The friction of the surface of the balance beam or the floor mat makes turning difficult. Gymnasts should perform all turns on the toes and balls of their feet. A gymnast must learn to focus so that she lands the turn where she intended to stop.

A **pivot turn** is the most basic turn. It's a simple turn done with both feet up on their toes. Cathy starts facing one direction and, when finished, faces the opposite direction.

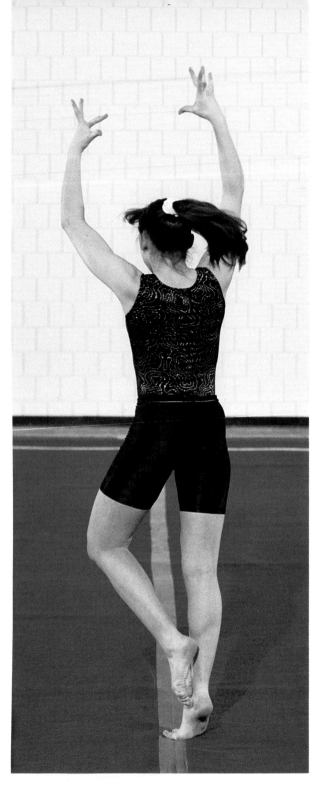

The **full turn** is a required skill in floor exercise and balance beam routines. Kristy holds her arms up and steps forward onto the ball of one foot. Her free leg may be placed in any number of positions.

Generally, the closer Kristy's leg is to her body, the faster she will turn. As she looks straight ahead, she turns around on her base leg a full 360 degrees so that she faces the same direction as when she started.

● *Jumps*

A jump is a skill in which the gymnast leaves the floor from both feet and then lands on both feet simultaneously. While she is in the air, the gymnast's legs may be in many different positions. Some examples are illustrated by Sara's straddle jump, above, and Kristy's tuck jump, left.

● *Leaps*

Leaps are usually performed after a short run to make them dynamic. To execute a leap, a gymnast transfers her weight from one foot to the other as high as possible in the air. Several leaps are often done, one right after the other, to make a series.

Good leaping requires excellent leg strength and flexibility. The **split leap** Jill is doing is the most basic of all the leaps, but still is very challenging. The gymnast's legs should be parallel with the floor and absolutely straight at the height of the leap.

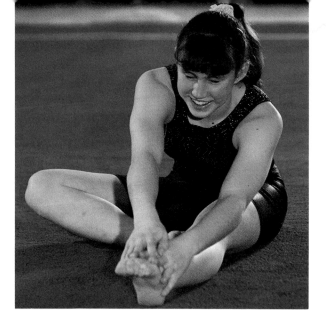

Typical Workout

The time gymnasts spend in the gym learning new skills, creating their competitive routines, and practicing is called a workout. Workout sessions will vary depending upon whether they take place before, during, or after the competitive season. Most workouts consist of three parts: warmup, rotations on apparatus, and conditioning.

● Warmup

No coach can overemphasize the importance of a proper warmup. During this time, gymnasts stretch, flex, and limber up their entire bodies. Correct techniques are required. These techniques will transfer to the skills the gymnasts perform later in the workout. A warmup usually takes place on the floor mat, but sometimes gymnasts will use the equipment or their teammates to help them warm up.

● Apparatus Practice

After the warmup, gymnasts divide into smaller groups to work on the apparatus. The time a gymnast spends at each event is called a rotation. Most people suggest there be no more than six to eight gymnasts for each coach while working on an apparatus. This ratio ensures adequate supervision and assistance for each individual.

The gymnasts go to different events for set periods of time during the workout session. Most coaches agree that regardless of whether a gymnast competes in every gymnastics event, he or she should work out regularly on each apparatus because of the transfer of skills that takes place between events.

● Conditioning

Finally, after the day's rotations are completed, there is time for conditioning. During this time, gymnasts do push-ups, sit-ups, splits, and sprints to increase the strength, flexibility, and endurance they need to execute skills better or to learn more skills.

Chapter 3.0

SHOWTIME

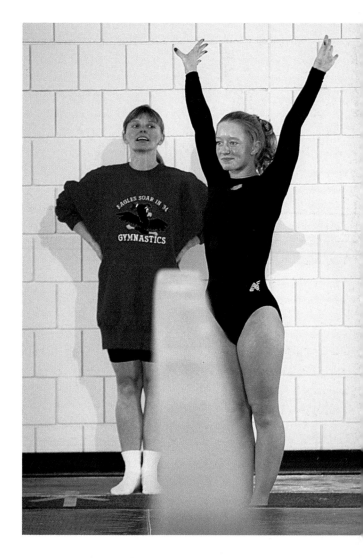

Jill is waiting for the green flag. In front of her awaits her biggest challenge of the day—the balance beam. In a few seconds, she will be up on that 4-inch beam that is even taller than she is. Soon she will be flipping, turning, dancing, and leaping. And, above all, Jill will be hoping she has prepared well so she will not fall.

Her coach whispers one last thought in her ear, "Do what you know you can do, Jill. You've got it!" There's the green flag. Jill raises her arms to **salute** the judge. And she's off! For a minute and a half, Jill is on top of that little piece of wood. The balance beam is her skinny stage. Let's find out how you can get involved in competitive gymnastics too.

Getting Started in Competition

Community recreation programs and YMCAs often have gymnastics classes. Sometimes, gymnastics instruction is available in school physical education classes. But most often, those wishing to be gymnasts take lessons at gymnastics clubs. Clubs usually offer gymnasts the chance to compete against athletes from other clubs.

Competitive opportunities are available at many different levels in the United States. If your goal is to be in the Olympics someday, you will want to compete in meets organized by USA Gymnastics (USAG) at the local, state, regional, and national levels. The USAG sets the requirements for competition that all member gymnasts and coaches must follow.

The USAG program is organized into levels. The lowest levels are noncompetitive and achievement oriented. They may be used within a school gym class or pre-team program. Competition begins in the middle levels. Gymnasts at these levels learn compulsory routines, which are routines that every gymnast must perform in competition.

In the advanced levels, gymnasts create their own routines, called optional routines. The routines must include some of the specific skills that are defined in the **Code of Points**, which is set by the **International Gymnastics Federation**.

Gymnasts compete against other gymnasts at the same level and in the same age group. To move up levels, gymnasts must show they have mastered specific skills. The gymnasts you see on television who represent the

United States in the Olympics or at other international meets have gone beyond these levels. These competitors are called elite gymnasts.

Some gymnastics clubs compete against each other outside of the USAG system. These independent clubs are usually not as strictly organized as USAG-sponsored programs.

Competition is also available at many junior and senior high schools. Sometimes gymnasts who started competing in a private club decide to join their school's gymnastics team. In this way, they can share the excitement of competition with their friends and represent their schools, too. The schools (and independent clubs) use the National Federation of High School Gymnastics rule book instead of the Code of Points for their competitions.

Many colleges across the nation have gymnastics teams. Some gymnasts may even receive scholarships to compete in gymnastics while attending college. College gymnasts usually have experience in high school or private club competition.

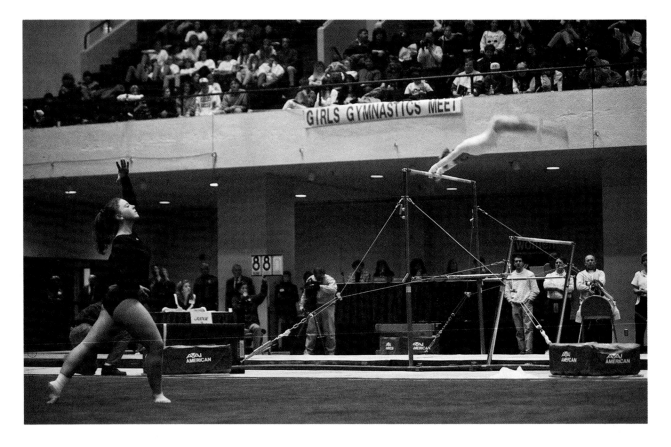

Getting Ready for a Meet

Preparing for a gymnastics meet is quite involved. First, there is the physical preparation. The gymnast must learn the skills that will be put into a routine. In USAG competition, the gymnast must compete in every event. When a gymnast does this, he or she is called an *all-arounder*. For most school and independent club competition, competing all-around is not required. When a gymnast chooses just one or a few events to compete in, he or she is called a *specialist.*

Once the basic skills are learned, they must be combined into a series of moves. In compulsory competition, these series or combinations are set. In optional competition, the combinations are unique to each gymnast. The gymnast and his or her coach decide on the skills and combinations from the Code of Points that best suit that gymnast's ability and style. The routines must be practiced and memorized so that they look polished.

For the floor exercise event, the gymnast must have the endurance to make it through the whole routine. The routine should look as easy to perform at the end as it did at the beginning when the gymnast was full of energy. Both the floor exercise and balance beam events are timed, so gymnasts in these events must also practice their timing so that they don't perform their routine too quickly or too slowly.

Judging

During a meet, each team is allowed to have a certain number of competitors in each event. Usually, two judges evaluate each routine in each event. For important competitions, there are sometimes as many as four judges.

The judges are looking for a performance that is as close to perfection as possible. Each routine is judged on a 10.0 scale. No matter what level of competition, all routines are worth 10 points if performed perfectly. Points or tenths of a point are deducted for mistakes. The 10 possible points are awarded based on difficulty of the skills (both required and optional), the composition of the routine, and the execution of the skills. Judges give bonus points to gymnasts who perform difficult maneuvers that weren't required in the routine.

Judges follow the rule book when evaluating each routine. But some of what the judge decides is based on his or her opinion. Routines must show confidence, originality, and be exciting to watch. Opinions about these qualities vary from one judge to another. Judges do confer when they don't agree. When the routine is scored by more than one judge, the final score is the average of the judges' scores.

Mental Preparation

The gymnast must also be prepared psychologically for competition. Mental and emotional training help a gymnast become ready to perform the physical skills.

When you watch gymnastics, you may wonder, "How does she do that?" and "Won't he get hurt?" A gymnast often fears that he or she may be injured. Many coaches believe that overcoming the fear of getting hurt is even more important than learning the skills.

Coaches spot, or physically assist, gymnasts while they do maneuvers until the coach is confident that there is very little chance that the gymnast will get hurt. And, coaches don't let a gymnast use a skill in competition unless the gymnast has first practiced it many, many times. People often say, "Practice makes perfect," but gymnastics coaches say, "Perfect practice makes perfect."

Gymnasts must also deal with the fear or anxiety they may feel when performing their routines in front of an audience. When a gymnast is nervous, he or she is more likely to make mistakes that can lead to an injury.

Gymnastics is often thought of as an individual sport, but competition also takes place between teams. There is, then, a lot of pressure to perform well for teammates and fans. A gymnast might feel that a fall would cost his or her team a victory.

Coaches have to find ways to help their gymnasts work through all of these psychological barriers. Many coaches ask their gymnasts to think about their gymnastics outside, as well as inside, of the gym. Sometimes coaches suggest gymnasts visualize, or imagine, doing their routines perfectly before they go to sleep or right before they compete. Some gymnasts keep a training notebook or journal to record their individual progress, problems, frustrations, and accomplishments. Their coaches read these notebooks and give the gymnasts feedback about how to improve. There's no doubt about it—gymnastics is as much a mental as a physical sport.

Safety First

Coaches have a responsibility to provide a safe environment in which to learn gymnastics skills. Everything must be checked and rechecked so there is little risk. The gymnasium should have the most up-to-date equipment possible. There should be ample room in between pieces of equipment and enough protective matting for the falls that occur during the learning process.

A gymnast must be ready—physically, mentally, and emotionally—to perform skills safely. A coach must have the knowledge, technique, and physical ability to teach and spot those skills.

RAZZLE DAZZLE

The goal of many gymnasts is to compete for a gymnastics team and, perhaps, one day to participate in the Olympic Games. To do that, gymnasts must train for many years, avoid injuries as much as possible, and learn advanced skills. Advanced moves come in handy once gymnasts begin to create their own optional routines.

Even if you don't plan on competing in the Olympics, you might enjoy learning new and more difficult maneuvers. Ask your coach for help in learning these skills and remember to always have a spotter when you are working on a new move.

Shannon Miller led the U.S. team to a gold medal in the 1996 Olympics and won an individual gold in the balance beam competition.

For floor exercise routines, gymnasts must learn to do somersaults, such as the back somersault Stacy is doing. Once a gymnast can do front and back flips in the tuck position, he or she can add variations.

Beth shows one such variation as she straightens and splits her legs in this **layout stepout** back flip.

In vaulting, advanced work requires adding twists or somersaults in the postflight. One popular advanced vault is a tsukahara, which is a quarter or half turn onto the horse followed by a back somersault. The vault may be done in the tuck, pike or layout position, with or without adding twists.

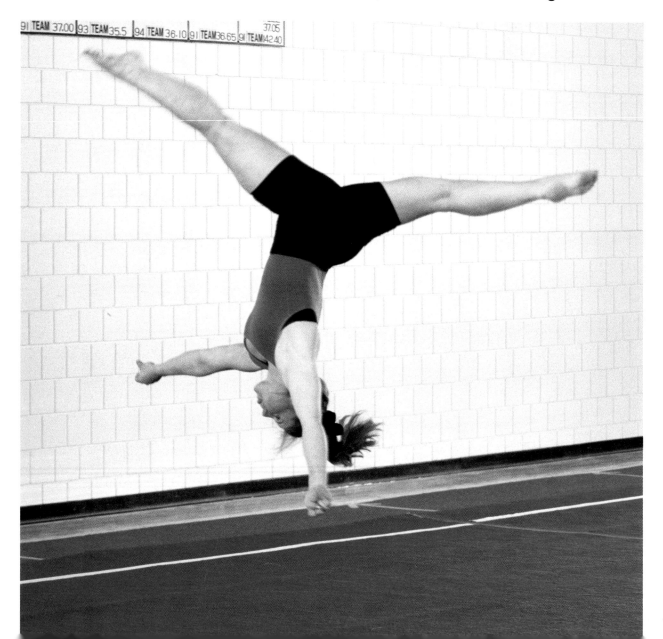

Advanced skills on both the boys'
high bar and girls' uneven parallel bars
usually include letting go of the bar in
mid-air and then quickly re-grasping it.
One such move is Sara's counter.

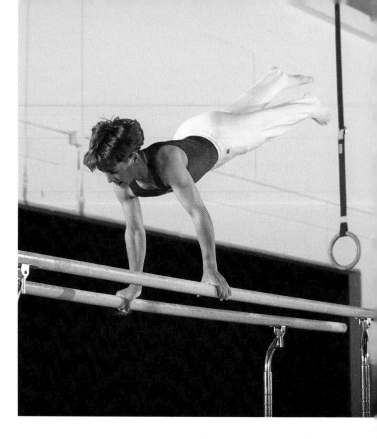

The parallel bars event is unique to boys' gymnastics. Pat is demonstrating a stütz. Pat swings through the bars and releases both hands. He then twists and grabs the bars—and is facing the opposite way from the direction he was originally facing.

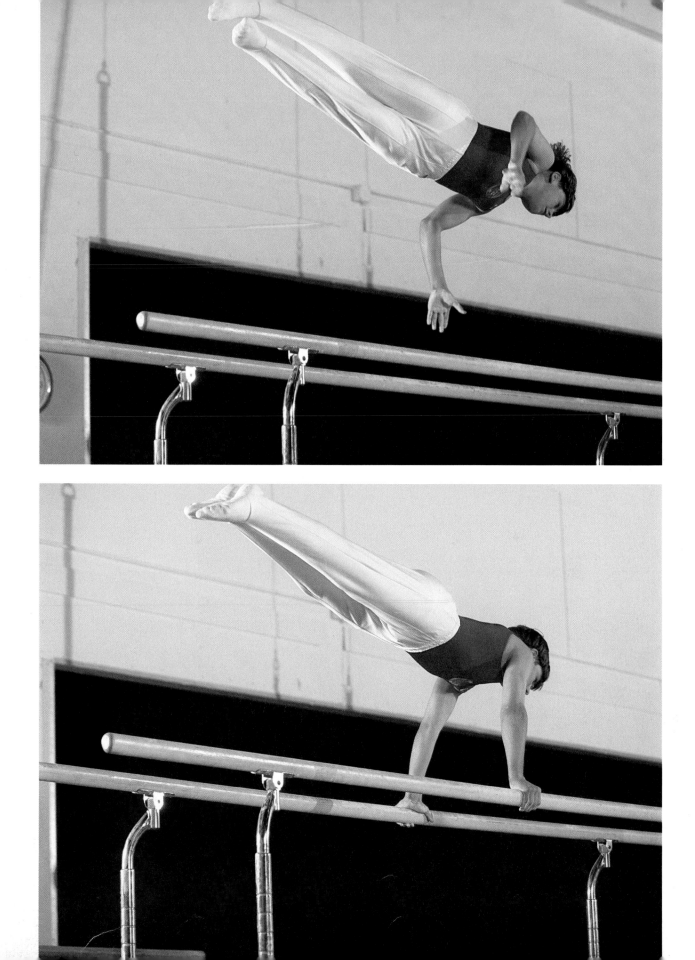

Jill needs control and flexibility when performing her **needle scale** on the balance beam. Gymnasts performing on the rings also use those qualities in many of their advanced moves.

Tony's **scissors** work on the pommel horse requires as much delicacy and accuracy as the back handspring on the beam that Kristy uses (on the next page) to lead into her dismount off the beam.

For her dismount off the beam, Kristy jumps backward onto her hands in a back handspring. As she lands back on her feet, she immediately pushes off again. Her momentum gives her extra height as she tucks into a back somersault dismount off the beam. She sticks the landing.

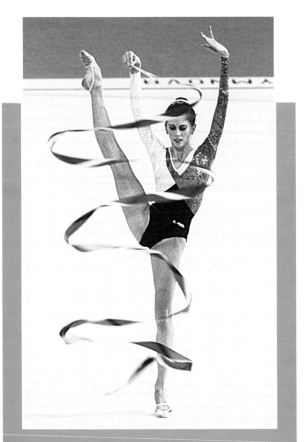

Rhythmic gymnasts use balls, ribbons, and hoops to create special effects.

Gymnastic Cousins

The six boys' and four girls' gymnastics events described in this book are called artistic gymnastics. Rhythmic gymnastics, acrogymnastics, and sports acrobatics are variations of gymnastics that are perhaps not as well known but are equally exciting.

Only girls and women compete in rhythmic gymnastics, which is an Olympic sport. Rhythmic gymnastics emphasizes grace, coordination, control, and poise. Gymnasts perform floor exercise routines that don't include tumbling moves. Instead, they use a ribbon, ball, hoop, club, or rope. The gymnasts perform leaps, jumps, turns, steps, waves, and other dance moves.

Acrogymnastics events include trampoline, double mini-trampoline, synchronized trampoline, and power tumbling. Acrogymnasts compete on local, regional, national, and international levels.

In sports acrobatics, pairs and groups of gymnasts perform routines of tumbling and balancing moves. The performers balance on and somersault from their partners.

Gymnastics is a complex sport in which athletes strive for perfection while trying to make their effort look as easy as possible. It is a sport that constantly changes, continually challenges, and will always be breathtaking to watch at any level.

GYMNASTICS TALK

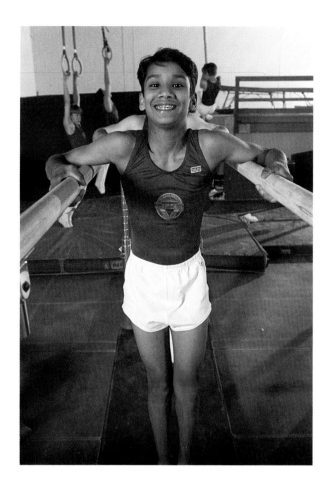

apparatus: The equipment used in the gymnastics events, specifically: uneven parallel bars, horizontal bar, rings, pommel horse, vault, parallel bars, and balance beam.

back handspring: A jump backward onto the hands, followed by a quick push from the hands to the feet. Also called flip-flop or flick-flack.

balance beam: A wooden or aluminum beam, 4 inches wide, 16 feet, 5 inches long, raised on metal supports 3 feet, 11 inches high. Girls perform timed routines on the beam.

block: The motion during which a gymnast changes from vertical to horizontal movement by preventing his or her shoulders from moving forward when in a hand support position or by preventing the hips from moving forward in the lunge position.

body wave: A technique involving successive movements of the arms or the whole body.

cartwheel: A rotation of the gymnast's body sideways through the upside down position on the hands and onto the feet, landing one foot at a time with straight legs.

circles: A circular movement of one or both legs on the pommel horse.

Code of Points: The international rule book used for judging gymnastic routines.

comaneci: A dismount from the uneven parallel bars performed by doing a circle off the top bar followed by a quarter twist and back flip.

dips: A conditioning exercise during which a gymnast supports his or her body on the parallel bars and raises and lowers himself or herself to build up arm strength.

dismount: A means of leaving the apparatus at the completion of a routine.

floor exercise: A timed gymnastics event performed on a mat measuring 40 feet by 40 feet. Boys perform tumbling skills. Girls perform tumbling and dance skills to music.

front handspring: A forward jump onto the gymnast's hands with immediate rotation forward onto his or her feet.

front walkover: A movement rotating forward round the shoulder axis, with momentary hand support in the upside down position.

full turn: A rotation about the vertical plane of the body in dance. In tumbling, a rotation about the horizontal axis.

giant swing: A skill used on the high bar and uneven parallel bars where the fully extended body circles around the bar.

grips: Devices gymnasts wear on their hands to hold onto the apparatus better. Also called handguards.

handstand: A move in which the gymnast supports his or her body on his or her hands while upside down.

horizontal bar: A metal bar supported by metal poles on which boys perform routines. Also called a high bar.

hurdle: A hop step used to begin a tumbling skill.

International Gymnastics Federation: The governing body of international gymnastics. Also known as FIG after its French translation.

layout: The basic body position in which the gymnast's body is completely stretched out and extended.

layout stepout: A back somersault with the gymnast's legs split and extended.

lunge: A leaning-over position with one foot ahead of the other and the gymnast's weight mainly on his or her lead leg, which is bent.

mount: A method of getting onto the apparatus to start a routine.

needle scale: A balance pose used on the balance beam in which one leg supports the gymnast's body and the other points to the ceiling.

pancake: A body position in which the gymnast's upper body is piked over flat to his or her lower body.

parallel bars: A pair of wooden or fiberglass bars of the same height and parallel to each other which are supported by adjustable metal poles. Also called P-bars.

pike: A basic body position in which the gymnast's body is folded at the hips. The gymnast's arms and legs are held straight.

pivot turn: A half-turn on the balls of both feet.

pommel horse: A leather-covered wooden frame with a straight body and two handles, called pommels, screwed into it. Also called a side horse.

Nikki demonstrates a scale on the balance beam. This pose requires balance and control. Beam routines must show both qualities.

preflight: A phase of the vault during which the gymnast's body is in space, from the time his or her feet leave the board until the gymnast's hands touch the horse.

rings: A pair of stationary rings supported from ropes and straps. Also called still rings.

roll: A tucked position moving either forward or backward during which the gymnast starts and ends on his or her feet.

roundoff: A cartwheel variation in which the gymnast lands on both feet at the same time, facing the way he or she began.

salute: An arm signal by a gymnast to a judge that indicates that the gymnast is ready to begin his or her routine.

scissors: A move used on the pommel horse in which the legs extend and cross each other.

somersault: A 360-degree rotation of the gymnast's body about its horizontal axis with upward flight and without hand support. Also called a flip or salto or somi.

split leap: A dance skill in which the gymnast pushes off of one foot and transfers her weight from one leg to the other with both legs parallel to the floor at the height of the leap.

postflight: A phase of the vault during which the gymnast's body is in space, from the time the gymnast's hands leave the horse until his or her feet land on the mat.

spring floor: A type of floor exercise mat made with springs or foam blocks, wooden boards, a foam pad, and carpeting.

stick: The action of landing a dismount without taking a step or completing a beam routine without any falls.

straddle: A body position of straight legs held apart with a wide angle between them.

tsukahara: A type of vault in which the gymnast does a quarter or half twist onto the horse followed by a one and a-half back flip off.

tuck: The basic body position in which the gymnast's knees are bent up to his or her chest, which is rounded, and the gymnast's chin is in and down.

tumbling pass: A series of tumbling skills on the floor exercise event.

twist: To rotate about the body's vertical axis.

uneven parallel bars: A pair of wooden or fiberglass bars on metal supports. The bars are parallel to each other but one is higher than the other. Also called asymmetric bars.

uprights: The vertical poles that support the parallel and uneven parallel bars.

vault: A flat-surfaced, leather-covered rectangular structure on wooden supports. Also called a horse.

V-ups: A sit-up-like movement done with straight legs to strengthen the gymnast's abdominal muscles.

FURTHER READING

Conner, Bart. *Winning the Gold.* New York: Warner Books, Inc., 1985.

Feeney, Rik. *Gymnastics: A Guide for Parents and Athletes.* Indianapolis, Ind.: Masters Press, 1992.

Low, Trevor. *Gymnastics: Floor, Vault, Beam, and Bar.* England: Crowood Press, 1993.

Whitlock, Steve. *Make the Team: Gymnastics for Girls.* Boston, Mass.: The Time Inc. Magazine Company (Little, Brown and Company), 1991.

FOR FURTHER INFORMATION

International Gymnast Magazine
P. O. Box 721020
Norman, OK 73070
www.intlgymnast.com

International Gymnastics Hall of Fame
120 North Robinson
Oklahoma City, OK 73102

USA Gymnastics
201 S. Capital Suite 300
Pan Am Plaza
Indianapolis, IN 46225
www.usa-gymnastics.org

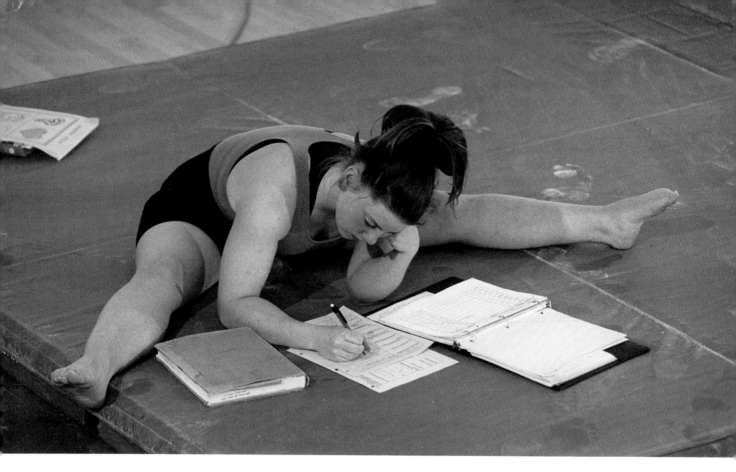

INDEX